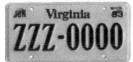    

Across the States

Activities · Games · Sticker Book

TABLE OF CONTENTS

Written by
Che Rudko

Illustrations by
David Brion

10 9 8 7 6 5 4 3 2 1

NEW ENGLAND STATES

The area in which the Mayflower Pilgrims first settled, New England is steeped in early American history. Today, the region attracts tourists interested not only in its many historic sites, but also hikers, skiers, fishermen, whale-watchers, and "leaf peepers" who come to see the brilliant autumn foliage.

NEW HAMPSHIRE *"The Granite State"*
The 9th State – June 21, 1788
State Bird: Purple finch
State Flower: Purple lilac
State Tree: White birch

New Hampshire's Mt. Washington is the highest peak in the northeast.

VERMONT *"The Green Mountain State"*
The 14th State – March 4, 1791
State Bird: Hermit thrush
State Flower: Red clover
State Tree: Sugar maple

Lake Champlain is reputed to have its own "Loch Ness Monster" – nicknamed Champ.

CONNECTICUT *"The Constitution State"*
The 5th State – January 9, 1788
State Bird: American robin
State Flower: Mountain laurel
State Tree: White oak

Called "The Constitution State" because it had the first written constitution in the U.S.

RHODE ISLAND *"The Ocean State"*
The 13th State – May 29, 1790
State Bird: Rhode Island red
State Flower: Violet
State Tree: Red maple

Rhode Island is the smallest state – only 1,545 square miles.

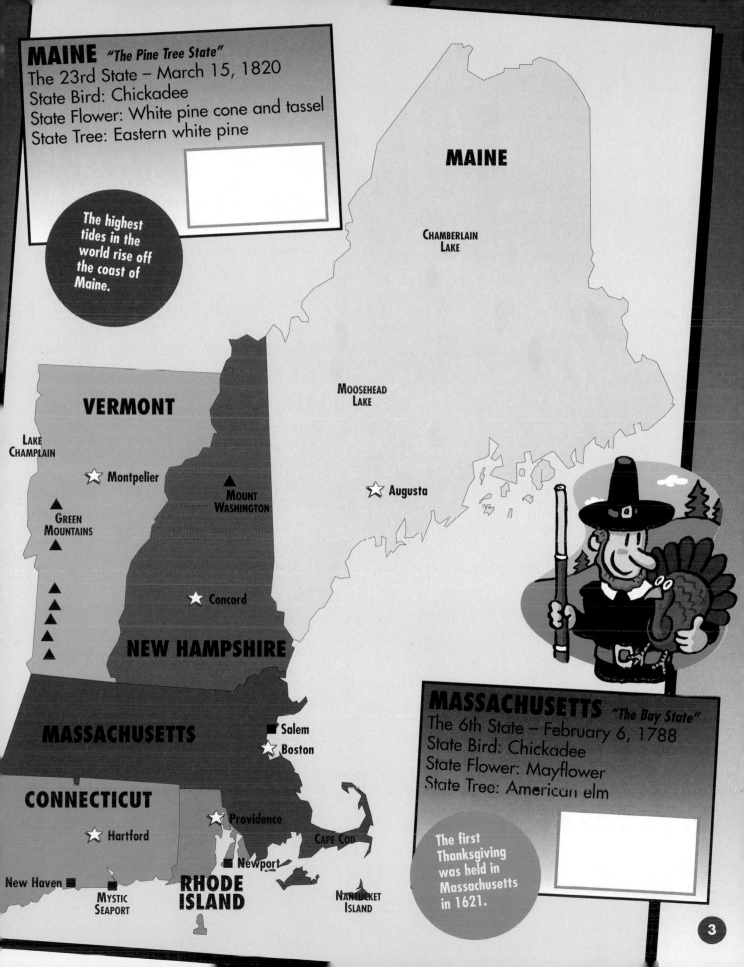

MAINE *"The Pine Tree State"*
The 23rd State – March 15, 1820
State Bird: Chickadee
State Flower: White pine cone and tassel
State Tree: Eastern white pine

The highest tides in the world rise off the coast of Maine.

MAINE

CHAMBERLAIN LAKE

MOOSEHEAD LAKE

☆ Augusta

VERMONT

LAKE CHAMPLAIN

☆ Montpelier

▲ MOUNT WASHINGTON

▲ GREEN MOUNTAINS

▲
▲
▲
▲
▲

☆ Concord

NEW HAMPSHIRE

MASSACHUSETTS

■ Salem
☆ Boston

CONNECTICUT

☆ Providence

☆ Hartford

CAPE COD

New Haven ■

■ Newport

■ MYSTIC SEAPORT

RHODE ISLAND

▲ NANTUCKET ISLAND

MASSACHUSETTS *"The Bay State"*
The 6th State – February 6, 1788
State Bird: Chickadee
State Flower: Mayflower
State Tree: American elm

The first Thanksgiving was held in Massachusetts in 1621.

3

MID-ATLANTIC STATES

Famous for the New York City metropolitan area, the mid-Atlantic states are less well-known for their rich farmlands and rambling mountain ranges, from the Adirondacks in northern New York State to the Appalachians in southern Pennsylvania. This area was, and continues to be, the "Gateway to America" for millions of immigrants who have come to live and work here.

PENNSYLVANIA "The Keystone State"
The 2nd State – December 12, 1787
State Bird: Ruffed grouse
State Flower: Mountain laurel
State Tree: Eastern hemlock

Hershey, Pennsylvania, is home to Hershey's Chocolate – the biggest chocolate factory in the world.

MARYLAND "The Old Line State"
The 7th State – April 28, 1788
State Bird: Baltimore oriole
State Flower: Black-eyed Susan
State Tree: White oak

Maryland has the only official state sport – ring jousting.

NEW JERSEY "The Garden State"
The 3rd State – December 18, 1787
State Bird: Eastern goldfinch
State Flower: Purple violet
State Tree: Red oak

The country's first organized baseball game was played in Hoboken in 1846.

■ Pittsburgh

DELAWARE "The Diamond State"
The 1st State – December 7, 1787
State Bird: Blue hen chicken
State Flower: Peach blossom
State Tree: American holly

Delaware native Caesar Rodney rode to Philadelphia to cast the deciding vote for the Declaration of Independence.

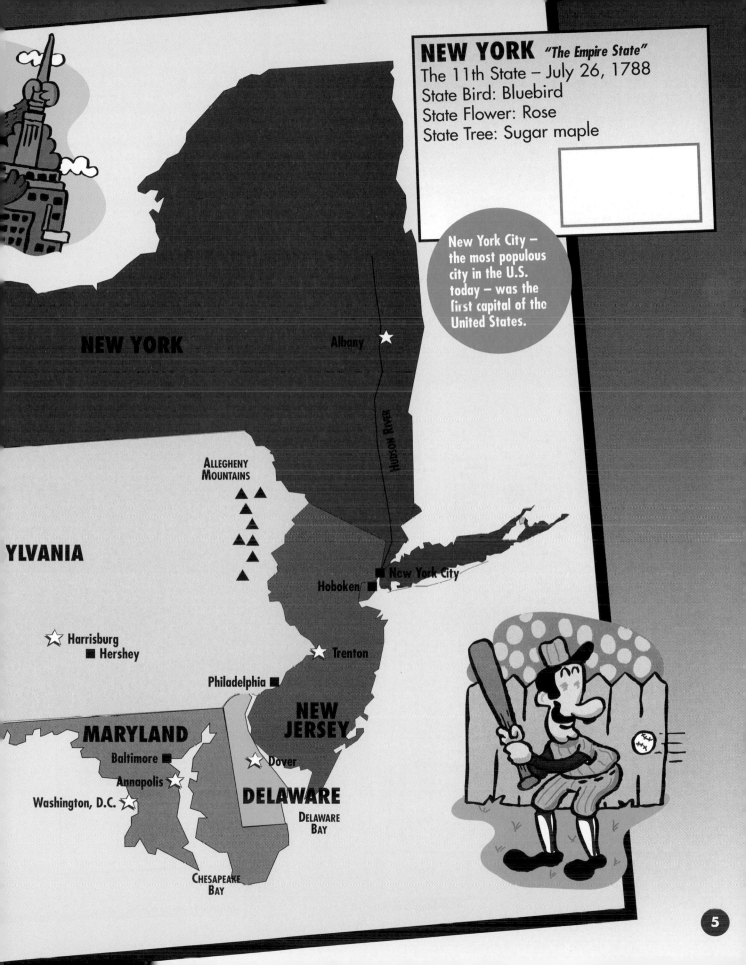

NEW YORK *"The Empire State"*
The 11th State – July 26, 1788
State Bird: Bluebird
State Flower: Rose
State Tree: Sugar maple

New York City – the most populous city in the U.S. today – was the first capital of the United States.

NEW YORK

Albany ☆

HUDSON RIVER

■ New York City

ALLEGHENY MOUNTAINS

■ Hoboken

YLVANIA

☆ Harrisburg
■ Hershey

☆ Trenton

Philadelphia ■

NEW JERSEY

MARYLAND

Baltimore ■

Annapolis ☆

Washington, D.C. ☆

☆ Dover

DELAWARE

DELAWARE BAY

CHESAPEAKE BAY

SOUTHERN STATES

Originally cultivated by slave labor, the South became the country's first great agricultural region. The South was ravaged by the Civil War, and struggled to rebuild its economy during the decades that followed. Today, while it continues to produce an abundance of tobacco, cotton, and rice, the South has also become a leader in such high-tech industries as aerospace research.

TENNESSEE *"The Volunteer State"*
The 16th State – June 1, 1796
State Bird: Mockingbird
State Flower: Iris
State Tree: Tulip poplar

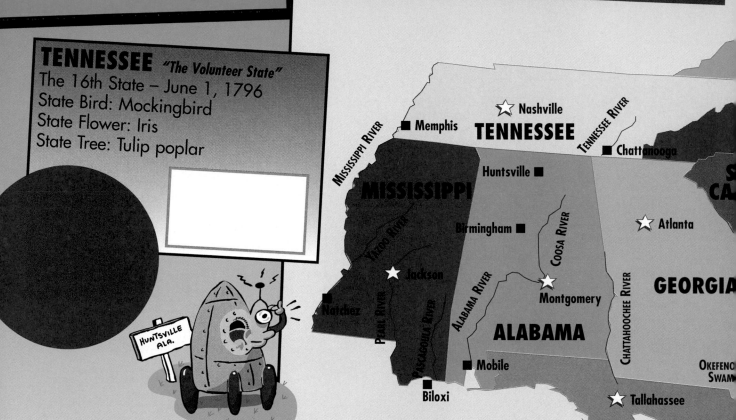

HUNTSVILLE ALA.

MISSISSIPPI *"The Magnolia State"*
The 20th State – December 10, 1817
State Bird: Mockingbird
State Flower: Magnolia
State Tree: Southern magnolia

The Pascagoula River is called the Singing River because it sometimes makes an unexplained humming sound.

ALABAMA *"The Heart of Dixie"*
The 22nd State – December 14, 1819
State Bird: Yellowhammer
State Flower: Camellia
State Tree: Southern pine

Huntsville, Alabama, is "Rocket City, U.S.A." – the national center for rocket and space vehicle research.

VIRGINIA *"The Old Dominion State"*
The 10th State – June 25, 1788
State Bird: Cardinal
State Flower: Dogwood flower
State Tree: Dogwood

Eight U.S. Presidents came from Virginia – more than any other state.

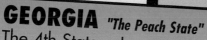

VIRGINIA

Washington, D.C.

Potomac River

Richmond

Kitty Hawk

Raleigh

Charlotte

NORTH CAROLINA

Cape Hattaras

Columbia

Fort Sumter

Savannah

Blackbeard's Island

Cape Canaveral

Miami

The Everglades

The Keys

Kitty Hawk, North Carolina, is the site of the Wright Brothers first flight on December 17, 1903 – the first airplane flight in history.

NORTH CAROLINA *"The Tar Heel State"*
The 12th State – November 21, 1789
State Bird: Cardinal
State Flower: Dogwood
State Tree: Long leaf pine

GEORGIA *"The Peach State"*
The 4th State – January 2, 1788
State Bird: Brown thrasher
State Flower: Cherokee rose
State Tree: Live oak

Blackbeard the Pirate made his headquarters on "Blackbeard Island" on the Georgia coast in the early 1700's.

SOUTH CAROLINA *"The Palmetto State"*
The 8th State – May 23, 1788
State Bird: Carolina wren
State Flower: Yellow jessamine
State Tree: Palmetto

The first shots of the Civil War were fired at Fort Sumter in S.C. on April 12, 1861.

FLORIDA *"The Sunshine State"*
The 27th State – March 3, 1845
State Bird: Mockingbird
State Flower: Orange blossom
State Tree: Sabal palmetto palm

Walt Disney World in Orlando, Florida, is the number one tourist attraction in the U.S.

GREAT LAKES STATES

The "Rust Belt," as it has been nick-named, forms the industrial heartland of the United States. Steel mills, lumber mills, auto factories, and meat processing plants are just a few of the industries that thrive in this region. The rich soil in the area has also made it a chief producer of corn, live-stock, and dairy products.

WISCONSIN *"The Badger State"*
The 30th State – May 29, 1848
State Bird: Robin
State Flower: Wood violet
State Tree: Sugar maple

Wisconsin produces 40% of the cheese eaten in the United States!

ILLINOIS *"The Prairie State"*
The 21st State – December 3, 1818
State Bird: Cardinal
State Flower: Native violet
State Tree: White oak

Chicago, Illinois, is home to the world's busiest airport – O'Hare – and the world's tallest building – the Sears Tower.

INDIANA *"The Hoosier State"*
The 19th State – December 11, 1816
State Bird: Cardinal
State Flower: Peony
State Tree: Tulip poplar

Wabash, Indiana, was the first electrically lighted city in the United States.

KENTUCKY *"The Bluegrass State"*
The 15th State – June 1, 1792
State Bird: Cardinal
State Flower: Goldenrod
State Tree: Kentucky coffee tree

Louisville, Kentucky, produces the world-famous "Louisville Slugger" baseball bats.

WEST VIRGINIA *"The Mountain State"*
The 35th State – June 20, 1863
State Bird: Cardinal
State Flower: Rhododendron
State Tree: Sugar maple

West Virginia was once part of Virginia, but was "born" during the Civil War when it refused to secede.

MISSISSIPPI RIVER

MISSISSIPPI R.

ILLINOIS R.

MADE IN LOUISVILLE

MICHIGAN *"The Wolverine State"*
The 26th State – January 26, 1837
State Bird: Robin
State Flower: Apple blossom
State Tree: White pine

Michigan has 3,177 miles of shoreline – more than any state except Alaska.

OHIO *"The Buckeye State"*
The 17th State – March 1, 1803
State Bird: Cardinal
State Flower: Scarlet carnation
State Tree: Buckeye

The hot dog was invented in Niles, Ohio, by Harry M. Stevens.

WISCONSIN

UPPER PENINSULA

LAKE SUPERIOR

LAKE HURON

Green Bay ■

LOWER PENINSULA

Madison ☆

■ Milwaukee

LAKE MICHIGAN

MICHIGAN

☆ Lansing

Chicago ■

Detroit ■

LAKE ERIE

■ Gary

ILLINOIS

Toledo ■

■ Cleveland

Springfield

INDIANA

OHIO

■ Weirton

☆ Indianapolis

☆ Columbus

■ Wheeling

WABASH RIVER

■ Cincinnati

OHIO RIVER

WEST VIRGINIA

☆ Louisville

☆ Frankfort

OHIO RIVER

FORT KNOX

☆ Charleston

ALLEGHENY MOUNTAINS

MAMMOTH CAVE

KENTUCKY

OHIO

9

SOUTHERN-
CENTRAL
STATES

From bayou to dustbowl, the South Central states are a region as diverse in their history as their landscape. Louisiana and Arkansas, originally settled by the French, joined the Confederacy during the Civil War. Texas, once a part of Mexico, was an independent Republic for ten years before becoming a state. Oklahoma was established as "Indian Territory" in the 1830s — an area where Southeastern tribes were forced to relocate — and was still called that until it became a state in 1907.

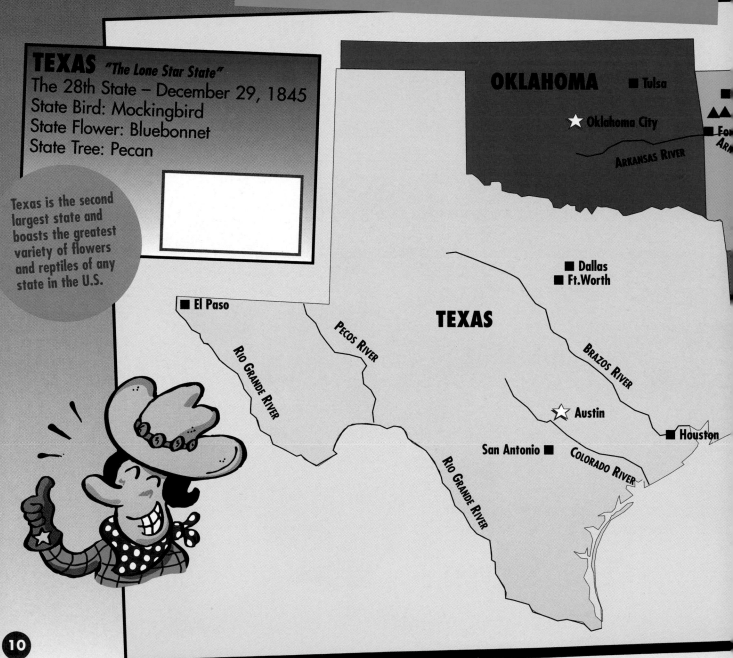

TEXAS *"The Lone Star State"*
The 28th State – December 29, 1845
State Bird: Mockingbird
State Flower: Bluebonnet
State Tree: Pecan

Texas is the second largest state and boasts the greatest variety of flowers and reptiles of any state in the U.S.

OKLAHOMA   ■ Tulsa

★ Oklahoma City

■ For
AR

ARKANSAS RIVER

■ El Paso

PECOS RIVER

RIO GRANDE RIVER

TEXAS

■ Dallas
■ Ft.Worth

BRAZOS RIVER

☆ Austin

■ Houston

San Antonio ■   COLORADO RIVER

RIO GRANDE RIVER

OKLAHOMA *"The Sooner State"*
The 46th State – November 16, 1907
State Bird: Scissor-tailed flycatcher
State Flower: Mistletoe
State Tree: Redbud

Oklahoma was once home to five separate American Indian nations.

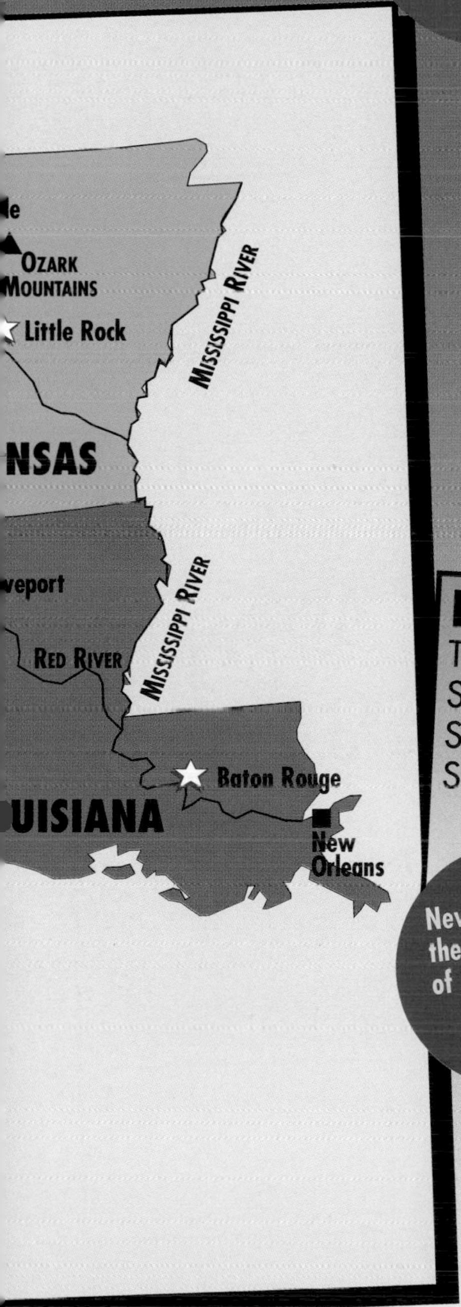

Ozark Mountains

★ Little Rock

MISSISSIPPI RIVER

NSAS

veport

RED RIVER

MISSISSIPPI RIVER

UISIANA

★ Baton Rouge

■ New Orleans

ARKANSAS *"The Land of Opportunity"*
The 25th State – June 15, 1836
State Bird: Mockingbird
State Flower: Apple blossom
State Tree: Pine

Arkansas is home to the American continent's only diamond mine.

LOUISIANA *"The Pelican State"*
The 18th State – April 30, 1812
State Bird: Brown pelican
State Flower: Magnolia
State Tree: Bald cypress

New Orleans is the "Birthplace of Jazz."

CENTRAL PLAINS STATES

Often referred to as "The Breadbasket" of the United States, the Central Plains provide most of the country's corn, wheat, and barley, as well as a huge amount of other agricultural products and livestock. This large area of fertile farmland is fed by the great Mississippi and Missouri River systems.

SOUTH DAKOTA *"The Coyote State"*
The 40th State – November 2, 1889
State Bird: Chinese ring-necked pheasant
State Flower: Pasque flower
State Tree: Black Hills spruce

The Homestake Mine in South Dakota has produced more gold than any other in the Americas.

MISSOURI

▲▲ MT. RUSHMOR

BLACK HILLS

PLATTE RIVER

NEBRASKA *"The Cornhusker State"*
The 37th State – March 1, 1867
State Bird: Western meadowlark
State Flower: Goldenrod
State Tree: Cottonwood

Nebraska is the only state whose nickname derives from its college football team – the Cornhuskers.

KANSAS *"The Sunflower State"*
The 34th State – January 29, 1861
State Bird: Western meadowlark
State Flower: Sunflower
State Tree: Cottonwood

Smith County, Kansas, contains the geographic center of the 48 contiguous United States.

MISSOURI *"The Show Me State"*
The 24th State – August 10, 1821
State Bird: Bluebird
State Flower: Hawthorn
State Tree: Dogwood

St. Louis' Gateway Arch is the country's tallest monument.

NORTH DAKOTA *"The Peace Garden State"*
The 39th State – November 2, 1889
State Bird: Western meadowlark
State Flower: Wild prairie rose
State Tree: American elm

The geographic center of North America lies in Rugby, North Dakota.

MINNESOTA *"The North Star State"*
The 32nd State – May 11, 1858
State Bird: Common loon
State Flower: Pink-and-white lady's slipper
State Tree: Red pine

Minnesota is the source of the Mississippi River and home to more than 15,000 lakes.

IOWA *"The Hawkeye State"*
The 29th State – December 28, 1846
State Bird: Eastern goldfinch
State Flower: Wild rose
State Tree: Oak

Iowa produces one-fifth of the U.S.'s corn, and is home to the country's biggest popcorn-packing plant.

Minot
■ Rugby

NORTH DAKOTA
☆ Bismarck
Fargo ■

MINNESOTA

LAKE SUPERIOR

SOUTH DAKOTA
☆ Pierre

MISSISSIPPI RIVER

☆ St. Paul
Minneapolis ■

MINNESOTA RIVER

MISSOURI RIVER

Sioux Falls ■

BRASKA

Sioux City ■

IOWA

MISSISSIPPI RIVER

Cedar Rapids ■

Omaha ■
☆ Des Moines

DES MOINES RIVER

☆ Lincoln

MISSOURI

Kansas City ■

KANSAS
☆ Topeka

MISSOURI RIVER

☆ St. Louis

MISSISSIPPI RIVER

▲ ▲
▲
Jefferson City ☆

OZARK MOUNTAINS

ge City
■ Wichita

IOWA POPCO

SOUTHWESTERN STATES

Though it contains lush green forests and farmlands, the Southwestern states are famous for their spectacular desert scenery and formations. The Southwest is also characterized by its Spanish/Mexican heritage and the Native American civilizations which first settled here. It is still home to the largest Native American population in the country.

⭐ **Carson City**

LAKE TAHOE

COLORADO *"The Centennial State"*
The 38th State – August 1, 1876
State Bird: Lark bunting
State Flower: Rocky Mountain columbine
State Tree: Colorado blue spruce

Thanks to the Rocky Mountains, Colorado has the highest average altitude of all fifty states.

UTAH *"The Beehive State"*
The 45th State – January 4, 1896
State Bird: Seagull
State Flower: Sego lily
State Tree: Blue spruce

Utah's Great Salt Lake – four times saltier than the Atlantic Ocean – is the largest salt lake in the country.

NEVADA *"The Silver State"*
The 36th State – October 31, 1864
State Bird: Mountain bluebird
State Flower: Sagebrush
State Tree: Single-leaf piñon

Nevada is a leading supplier of the world's turquoise and rare opals.

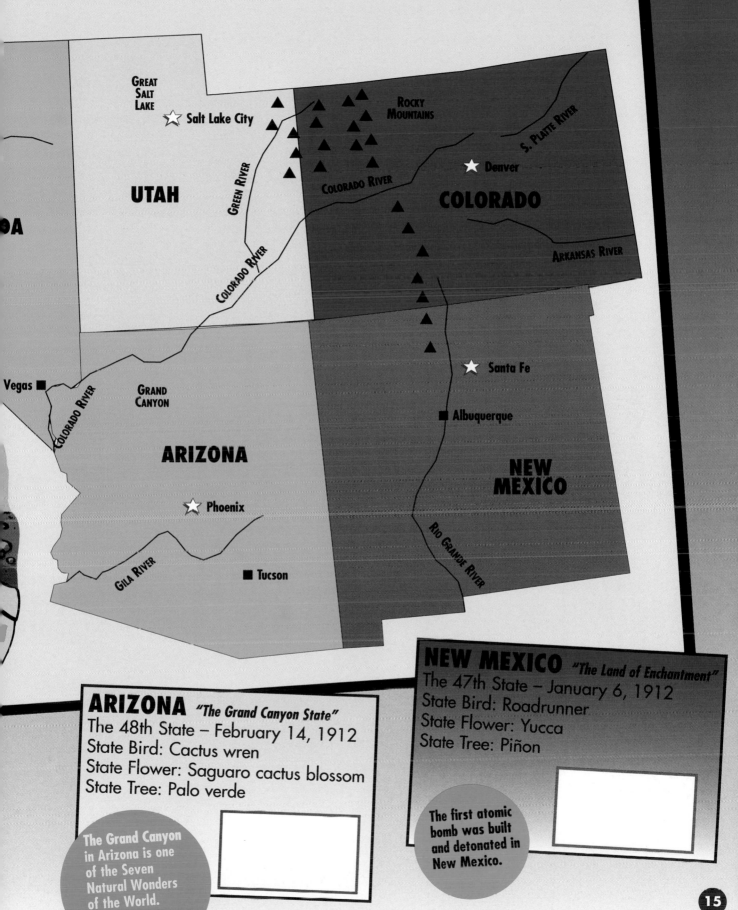

GREAT
SALT
LAKE

☆ Salt Lake City

ROCKY
MOUNTAINS

S. PLATTE RIVER

GREEN RIVER

UTAH

☆ Denver

COLORADO RIVER

COLORADO RIVER

COLORADO

ARKANSAS RIVER

Vegas ■

COLORADO RIVER

GRAND
CANYON

☆ Santa Fe

ARIZONA

■ Albuquerque

☆ Phoenix

NEW
MEXICO

GILA RIVER

■ Tucson

RIO GRANDE RIVER

NEW MEXICO *"The Land of Enchantment"*
The 47th State – January 6, 1912
State Bird: Roadrunner
State Flower: Yucca
State Tree: Piñon

ARIZONA *"The Grand Canyon State"*
The 48th State – February 14, 1912
State Bird: Cactus wren
State Flower: Saguaro cactus blossom
State Tree: Palo verde

The Grand Canyon
in Arizona is one
of the Seven
Natural Wonders
of the World.

The first atomic
bomb was built
and detonated in
New Mexico.

WESTERN GREAT PLAINS STATES

The Rocky and Bitteroot Mountains of the Western Plains provide some of the country's most breathtaking national parks. The foothills of the Rockies also provide grazing land for huge herds of cattle and, more recently, bison that have returned from near-extinction. The Western Plains are also rich ground for the mining of silver, copper, coal, and Black Hills gold.

DEVIL'S TOWER

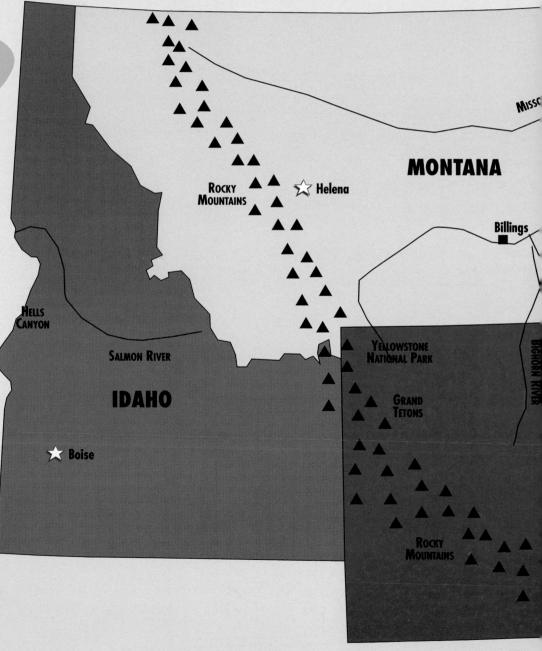

MISSO

MONTANA

Helena

Billings

ROCKY MOUNTAINS

HELLS CANYON

SALMON RIVER

IDAHO

Boise

YELLOWSTONE NATIONAL PARK

BIGHORN RIVER

GRAND TETONS

ROCKY MOUNTAINS

MONTANA *"The Treasure State"*
The 41st State – November 8, 1889
State Bird: Western meadowlark
State Flower: Bitterroot
State Tree: Ponderosa pine

Custer's Last Stand took place in Montana at the Little Big Horn in 1876.

IDAHO *"The Gem State"*
The 43rd State – July 3, 1890
State Bird: Mountain bluebird
State Flower: Syringa
State Tree: White pine

Hell's Canyon in Idaho plunges to 1½ miles deep – the deepest gorge in North America.

ONE RIVER

DEVIL'S TOWER

MING

■ Casper

N. PLATTE RIVER

★ Cheyenne

WYOMING *"The Equality State"*
The 44th State – July 10, 1890
State Bird: Meadowlark
State Flower: Indian paintbrush
State Tree: Cottonwood

Home of Yellowstone National Park, Grand Teton National Park, Devil's Tower National Monument, and Hot Springs State Park.

WEST COAST STATES

The Pacific Coast states boast a remarkable variety of natural beauty, from the sand dunes of Death Valley in Southern California to the temperate rain forest in Washington. The "left coast" is also known for its frequent earthquakes and, in the case of Mt. St. Helens in Washington, its less frequent volcanic eruptions.

OREGON "The Beaver State"
The 33rd State – February 14, 1859
State Bird: Western meadowlark
State Flower: Oregon grape
State Tree: Douglas fir

Crater Lake in Oregon is 1,932 feet deep — the deepest lake in the country.

CALIFORNIA "The Golden State"
The 31st State – September 9, 1850
State Bird: California valley quail
State Flower: Golden poppy
State Tree: California redwood

The largest living thing on earth, a tree called "General Sherman," stands in the Sequoia National Park of California.

WASHINGTON *"The Evergreen State"*

The 42nd State – November 11, 1889
State Bird: Willow goldfinch
State Flower: Rhododendron
State Tree: Western hemlock

Washington leads the world in the production of apples.

NON-CONTIGUOUS STATES

Of the 50 states, 48 are "contiguous"— or touch each other. The other two, Alaska and Hawaii, are separated from the "lower 48" by Canada (in the case of Alaska) and the Pacific Ocean (in the case of Hawaii).

These two states could hardly be less alike! The nation's only island-state, small Hawaii is world-famous for its lush tropical plant-life, warm beaches, and bubbling volcanoes. Alaska, the largest state, is also the country's coldest, posting temperatures near –70° F in the winter months. It is also the most sparsely populated of all the states, but it can claim sizable populations of polar bears, walruses, and caribou.

ARCTIC OCEAN

ALASKA

BERING STRAIT

YUKON RIVER

Fairbanks ■

MT. McKINLEY

BERING SEA

Anchorage ■

Juneau ★

KAUAI

OAHU

Honolulu ★

MAUI

MOLOKAI

LANAI

KALOOLAWE

HAWAII

HAWAII

HAWAII VOLCANOES NATIONAL PARK

ALASKA *"The Last Frontier"*

The 49th State – January 3, 1959
State Bird: Willow ptarmigan
State Flower: Forget-me-not
State Tree: Sitka spruce

Alaska is the largest state and is one-fifth the size of all the other states put together.

HAWAII *"The Aloha State"*

The 50th State – August 21, 1959
State Bird: Nene (Hawaiian Goose)
State Flower: Red hibiscus
State Tree: Kukui (candlenut)

Hawaii is home to the most active volcano in the world – Kilauea crater on Mauna Loa.

WASHINGTON

MONTANA

OREGON

IDAHO

WYOMING

NEVADA

UTAH

COLORADO

CALIFORNIA

ARIZONA

NEW MEXICO

LICENSE PLATE DOMINOES

HOW TO PLAY:
Shuffle the license plate stickers and distribute them equally among two or more players. The first player then places his/her sticker on a state. Subsequent players must place their stickers on states that adjoin it. Play continues until no further moves can be made. The player able to dispense the most stickers wins.

STATE
QUESTIONS

1. Which of the 13 original colonies was the first to become a state in the new United States of America?

2. In which state were both the Declaration of Independence and Constitution written?

3. In which state could you drive on the Garden State Parkway?

4. General Sherman burned Atlanta on his march through this state.

5. The state song of this "constitution state" is "Yankee Doodle."

6. Which state held the notorious Salem Witch Trials?

7. The Chesapeake Bay retriever was developed in this state – the only one to develop a distinct dog breed.

8. The Civil War began in this state.

9. This state has the shortest coastline of any that touches an ocean.

10. Richmond in this state was the capital of the Confederacy during the Civil War.

11. In which state would you visit the American side of Niagra Falls?

12. This "tar-heel" state leads the country in tobacco production.

13. Which of the original 13 colonies was the last to become a state?

14. Which is the only northeast corner state with no Atlantic coastline?

15. This state is also known as "The Bluegrass State."

16. Elvis Presley's home, Graceland, is in the musical capital of this state.

17. The Rock and Roll Hall of Fame is located in Cleveland in this state.

18. The mouth or "delta" of the Mississippi River is in this state.

19. In which state do Hoosiers reside?

20. Over 500 pre-Civil War mansions are said to stand in Natchez in this state.

21. Abraham Lincoln lived in the capital Springfield of this state when he was elected President.

22. The rocket that put man on the moon was designed here

23. And launched here.

24. This state is the eastern-most point in the United States.

25. St. Louis in this state is the world's largest shoe manufacturing center.

26. This "diamond state" leads the nation in chicken production.

27. Which of these Great Lakes States is the only state in the U.S. consisting of two separate parts?

28. In this state you'll find the Alamo in San Antonio.

29. Herbert Hoover, the first President born west of the Mississippi River, was born in this, the 29th state.

30. The "badgers" of this state were actually miners, not animals.

31. Though many of its redwoods soar over 300 feet high, this state is also home to the lowest point in the United States, Death Valley – 282 feet below sea level.

32. The Twin Cities, Minneapolis/St. Paul, are home to the nation's largest shopping mall in this state.

33. This state might have been nicknamed "the Valentine's Day State."

34. Wild West figures like Wyatt Earp and Doc Holliday once walked the streets of Dodge City in this state.

35. The city of Weirton in this state is the only one in the country which extends from one state border to another – it's wedged in between Ohio and Pennsylvania.

36. Based on the date of its statehood, which of these states might also be called "The Halloween State?"

37. This cornhusking state is the birthplace of Arbor Day.

38. The capital of this state is nicknamed "The Mile-High City."

39. In 1932 the International Peace Garden was dedicated on the border of this state to symbolize friendship between the U.S. and Canada.

40. Mt. Rushmore in this state displays the world's largest portrait busts.

41. Among the "treasures" unearthed in this state have been dinosaur bones.

42. This is the only state named after a president.

43. Potatoes are the true "gem" of this state – it grows ⅔ of all those eaten in the U.S.

44. Proud of its tradition of equality, this state was the first to give women the right to vote, and the first to elect a woman governor.

45. Rainbow Bridge, the nation's highest and largest natural arch, is found in this salty state.

46. Because of its shape, this state has been compared to a meat cleaver.

47. Santa Fe in this state is the oldest capital city in the U.S.

48. The last of the contiguous states to join the Union.

49. This state was purchased from Russia in 1867 for 7.2 million dollars – less than 2¢ an acre.

50. This is the only state not on the North American continent.